RISE™
Identity & Worth
Journal

RISE

Rooted ❖ Intentional ❖ Strong ❖ Energized™

A transformational book series

exploring balance, belief, and embodied wellness.

RISE™

Identity & Worth

Journal

A 12-Week Journey to a
Rooted, Intentional, Strong, and Energized Life
Volume 1

Angel Tate Keaton

Healthy in Heart Media™, LLC

Roanoke, VA

Published in the United States of America by

Healthy in Heart Media™, LLC

P.O. Box 694

Vinton, VA 24179

Copyright © 2026 by Angel Tate Keaton

First Printing January 2026

Cover art and design by the author

ISBN— 978-1-969064-17-3

Trademark Notice

RISE Rooted, Intentional, Strong, Energized™, and related marks and program names are trademarks of Healthy in Heart Media, LLC. Unauthorized use is prohibited.

Educational Purpose Notice

This guide is provided for personal development and educational use within RISE Circles. It may not be altered, repackaged, or redistributed as original training material.

Disclaimer

The author of this book does not dispense medical advice, mental-health diagnoses, or prescribe the use of any technique as a form of treatment for medical, emotional, psychological, or physical conditions. Any information contained in this book should not be used as a substitute for professional care or the guidance of a licensed physician, therapist, counselor, or qualified healthcare provider. The intent of the author is solely to offer information of a general, educational nature to support your personal journey toward emotional, physical, mental, and spiritual well-being.

If you choose to apply any of the practices or concepts presented in this book, you do so voluntarily and at your own discretion. The author and publisher assume no responsibility for your actions or for any consequences that may arise from the use or misuse of the information herein.

This guide is not clinical training and does not qualify or certify the reader to provide counseling, therapy, crisis intervention, or any form of licensed mental-health services. Facilitators using this material are responsible for maintaining healthy boundaries and referring individuals to professional care when needed.

No Guarantee of Outcomes

The practices, reflections, and strategies in this guide are intended to support whole-being wellness. Individual results will vary. The author or publisher guarantees no specific emotional, physical, or spiritual outcome.

Facilitator Responsibility Notice

This guide provides educational structure for peer-based wellness circles. It is not clinical training and does not certify the facilitator to provide professional counseling, therapy, crisis intervention, or any form of licensed mental-health care. Facilitators are responsible for maintaining appropriate boundaries and referring members to qualified professionals when needed. Healthy in Heart Media, LLC assumes no liability for how the material is used, interpreted, or implemented in any RISE Circle or group environment.

Group Safety & Confidentiality Notice

Facilitators and participants are responsible for creating a safe and respectful environment. Healthy in Heart Media, LLC is not responsible for any breaches of confidentiality, interpersonal conflict, or harm resulting from group interactions. Participation in any RISE Circle is voluntary, and all members are encouraged to seek professional support for concerns beyond the scope of this program.

Emergency Help Notice

This material is not intended for crisis situations. If you or a participant is experiencing a medical, mental-health, or safety emergency, contact local emergency services or a licensed professional immediately.

No Professional Relationship Notice

Reading this book does not establish a counseling, coaching, therapeutic, or professional relationship between the reader and the author or publisher. This material is for personal growth and educational use only and is not a substitute for individualized professional advice, diagnosis, or treatment.

Spiritual Disclaimer

Spiritual references and practices presented in this book reflect the author's personal faith and are offered for reflection, not as doctrinal instruction or religious authority.

Scripture Notice

Unless otherwise noted, all Scripture quotations are taken from the American Standard Version (ASV), as provided by BibleGateway.com. The American Standard Version was initially published in 1901 and is now in the public domain. This version was chosen for its consistent use of the divine name in the Old Testament and its closer alignment with the original Hebrew, making it a suitable foundation for a return-to-Eden perspective.

Dedication

For the one who has quietly carried more than anyone knows.

For the one learning to lay down old labels and step into truth.

For the one rebuilding their worth, breath by breath, choice by choice.

May these pages be a gentle place to return to yourself,

and a reminder that you were never unworthy—not for a moment.

For the brave one who is untangling old stories,

reframing the narratives that once defined you,

and choosing to believe that your life is worth healing.

May these pages hold your tears, your hope, your honesty,

and remind you:

>   You are more than what happened to you.

>   You are more than who others said you were.

>   Your true self is worth rediscovering.

Rise each day like the sun—
Rooted in truth,
Intentional in habits,
Strong in spirit, and
Energized for the hope of tomorrow.

~Angel Tate Keaton

When the phoenix burns,
It does not perish.
It rises from the ashes—refined.

Table of Contents

HOW TO USE THIS JOURNAL

A Gentle Guide for Your 12-Week Identity & Worth Journey

Welcome to the RISE™ Identity & Worth Journal.

These pages are designed to help you move slowly, intentionally, and compassionately through your story as you rediscover truth, reclaim identity, and rebuild worth from the inside out.

Each week follows a consistent rhythm so your body, mind, and spirit learn to settle into a predictable, safe pattern of reflection and renewal. The structure is simple, but deeply transformational when you move through it with honesty and kindness toward yourself.

Below is an overview of how each week is built.

1. Weekly Theme Page

Each week opens with a beautifully designed theme page that sets the tone for your journey.

Here you'll find:

> The Week Number & Weekly Theme, grounding your focus for the next seven days.
>
> A Clear Subtitle, giving you the lens through which we'll explore Identity & Worth that week.
>
> A Gentle Introduction, written to help you enter the topic with calm, clarity, and emotional safety.
>
> Reflective Artwork, chosen to visually echo the week's theme and create a sense of calm.

This page is meant to ease you into the week—helping your mind settle, your body soften, and your heart open to what this chapter will bring.

2. Weekly Inspiration

Each week opens with a simple, grounding moment to help you settle into the theme.

On this page you'll find:

A Weekly Inspiration Quote — chosen to reflect the week's focus on identity, worth, and wholeness.

A Quiet Reflection Box — a space to note the first thoughts, emotions, or intentions rising in you at the start of your week.

Gentle Visual Elements — minimal, calming artwork that sets a reflective tone.

This page acts like a deep breath — drawing you inward before the work of the week begins.

3. Awareness Check-In Page

Before you reflect with words, you'll begin with your body.

Each week, you'll use the same three grounding prompts to help you slow down, listen inward, and settle into the truth of the present moment.

You'll check in with:

Sensations — What is happening in your body (chest, shoulders, throat, stomach)?

Emotions — Which emotion is closest to the surface?

Needs — What is one need your heart or body is expressing today?

This practice invites your nervous system into the process and helps you journal from embodied awareness rather than only from your thoughts.

The prompts remain the same every week — because your body's truth changes as you do.

4. Core Journal Prompts

These prompts change weekly and explore:

Past labels

Emotional patterns

Core beliefs

Internal narratives

Worth, identity, and truth

The layout gives you structured space to process each prompt slowly and honestly.

These questions gently reveal what shaped you — and what you are ready to release or rewrite.

5. Diving Deeper Pages

After you finish the five core questions on Page 4, the *Diving Deeper* page gives you guided space to go further into the week's theme.

Each of the three sections on this page includes:

A targeted follow-up question designed to help you explore the topic from a deeper angle.

Lined space to process more personal, specific, or vulnerable reflections.

These questions are still connected to the main weekly theme, but they gently push you beyond surface-level answers. They help you:

Notice patterns or beliefs you may have overlooked

Explore why certain thoughts or reactions show up

Identify deeper layers of your identity, worth, or emotional landscape

Capture any insights that emerge later in the week

Use this page slowly. You might answer one question a day, revisit it mid-week, or spread it across the entire week—whatever supports your growth. These prompts are meant to deepen clarity, strengthen self-awareness, and help you uncover the truths you are uncovering as you walk through the RISE journey.

6. My Inner Dialog

This page is your open space to process anything that arises throughout the week—thoughts, emotions, prayers, questions, breakthroughs, or things you're still untangling. Unlike the guided prompts on the previous pages, this section is intentionally unstructured so you can write freely and honestly without limits.

Use this page to:

Capture thoughts that don't fit neatly into the weekly prompts

Journal through emotions that surface unexpectedly

Reflect on conversations, memories, or insights that feel important

Write prayers, declarations, or anything YHVH is revealing

Track patterns, moments of clarity, or internal shifts

There is no expectation and no "right way" here. Let this page hold your inner world just as it is—raw, real, and growing. This space is for your voice, your journey, and your unfolding story.

7. Release & Replace Page

This page guides you in releasing one internal label or belief each week and replacing it with truth.

The focus of this page changes depending on the weekly theme.

Each week, this page helps you:

> Name one belief, label, or internal narrative that has limited your sense of worth.
>
> Cross it out boldly inside the label box to visually release it.
>
> Write a truer, freer identity statement in the open journal area.
>
> Ground that truth in your body through writing, repetition, and imagery.

For Week 1, you release an old identity label.

In later weeks, this page may guide you to release:

> Shame
>
> Fear
>
> Old roles
>
> Comparison
>
> Self-criticism
>
> Or any other distortion that blocks your worth

Every week, you'll be invited to let go of what no longer serves you and replace it with what aligns with who you truly are.

8. Identity or Truth Statements Page

This page appears every week and guides you deeper into identity alignment.

Each week's focus shifts slightly based on the chapter theme, but the structure stays the same.

On this page you will:

> Write 5 identity statements rooted in truth

These are "I am…" statements that reflect who you are beneath labels, fear, or old patterns.

Each week's prompt will be adjusted to match the chapter focus — but always in the direction of truth and worth.

Write 5 "I am becoming…" statements

These help you grow toward the identity you're cultivating.

They encourage movement, healing, and forward expansion rather than perfection.

Choose one Anchoring Truth for the week

This is a single grounding sentence that helps direct your thinking and emotions.

It's the truth you will carry into your embodiment practice on the next page.

This page strengthens the identity you are growing into—one truth-filled statement at a time.

9. Embodiment Practice Page

Identity isn't just something you think — it's something you practice.

Every week, you will choose one new identity truth to embody and walk out.

This page guides you through four grounding steps:

This Week's Identity Truth

The one statement you want to carry, practice, or grow into this week.

What It Means to Me

Why this truth matters, what it represents, and how it shifts your story.

How I Will Practice It

Two prompts help you take it into daily life:

• How will I practice this truth in daily life?

• What reminder will ground me in this truth?

Return-to-Truth Plan

What will help me return to this truth on difficult days?

This page repeats each week — creating a rhythm where your nervous system can internalize truth through small, compassionate, consistent action..

10. End-of-Week Reflection

At the end of each week, you'll pause to observe what changed within you gently.

This page helps you look back with softness and clarity as you deepen integration.

You'll be guided through:

What shifted?

What felt hard?

What felt healing?

What surprised you?

What truth carried you?

What you are proud of yourself for

These prompts help you recognize growth, resilience, and progress—no matter how small—so that identity healing becomes embodied rather than rushed.

This page repeats every week, giving you a consistent rhythm of reflection.

11. Weekly Coloring Page

Each week ends with a beautiful botanical line illustration, giving your mind space to rest, process, and create.

Coloring:

Activates calm

Encourages reflection

Helps deepen emotional integration

Offers a peaceful close to the week

How to Move Through Each Week

Move slowly.

There is no rush.

If you need more than a week for a theme, take it.

If a page feels too tender today, come back when you're ready.

If something stirs emotion, pause and breathe.

This journal is not about fixing yourself — it is about finding yourself again.

Every entry is a step toward the truth.

Every breath is a step toward wholeness.

Every week is an invitation to rise.

BEFORE YOU BEGIN: IDENTITY IS FORMED BEFORE IT IS CHOSEN

You did not wake up one day and decide who you were.

Long before you had language for identity or worth, your nervous system was already learning what felt safe, what earned approval, and what needed to be hidden. Identity is formed in atmosphere — not intention.

We absorb names before we can question them.
We adapt before we understand.
We survive before we self-define.

This journal is not about reinventing yourself.
It is about uncovering who you became in response to life — and deciding what still belongs.

As you begin, hold this gently:

Some identities were formed to protect you.

Some beliefs helped you survive seasons you no longer live in.

Releasing them does not mean they were wrong — only that they are no longer required.

This is not a process of rejection.
It is a process of discernment.

THE DIFFERENCE BETWEEN IDENTITY, ROLE, AND CONDITIONING

Much of what we call "identity" is actually something else.

Roles are what we do.
Conditioning is what we learned.
Identity is who we are beneath both.

When roles change — parent, partner, caregiver, achiever, helper — many people experience disorientation, anxiety, or grief. This is not a weakness. It is a sign that identity and role have become intertwined.

Likewise, conditioning often disguises itself as truth:

- "I am responsible for everyone."
- "I am too much."
- "I am not enough."
- "I must earn rest, love, or belonging."

These are learned responses — not core identity.

This journal will help you:

- Separate who you are from what you do
- Notice where conditioning shaped self-worth
- Gently disentangle truth from adaptation
- Rebuild identity without removing compassion for your past

Nothing here asks you to abandon who you've been.
It asks you to clarify who you are now.

WORTH IS NOT PERFORMANCE, PROGRESS, OR PERCEPTION

Worth does not fluctuate — even when feelings do.

It is not determined by:

- Productivity
- Body size or health
- Emotional regulation
- Spiritual consistency
- Other people's approval
- Your ability to "do the work well."

Many people arrive at identity healing carrying a quiet fear:
"If I slow down, who am I without my effort?"

This journal intentionally slows the pace — not to take something from you, but to reveal what has always been present beneath striving.

Here, worth is treated as inherent, not earned.
Healing is allowed to be:

- Uneven
- Nonlinear
- Quiet
- Slow
- Incomplete

You are not proving anything in these pages.
You are remembering.

HOW TO HOLD YOURSELF THROUGH THIS JOURNEY

This work may surface emotion — not because something is wrong, but because something is being seen.

As you move forward:

- Pause when you feel overwhelmed
- Skip questions that feel too raw
- Return later without shame
- Let the body lead when words feel distant

You are allowed to:

- Write lightly or deeply
- Repeat the same truth for weeks
- Change your answers
- Take breaks
- Come back

Identity and worth are not rebuilt through force.
They are restored through safety, repetition, and truth held gently over time.

This journal is not here to demand transformation.
It is here to witness it.

What You'll Need Each Week

A Simple Guide for Your Identity & Worth Journey

Your RISE™ Identity & Worth journey is gentle and intentional. You don't need much to begin—just a few items and a willing heart. Here's what will help you get the most out of each week:

Practical Items

This journal — your safe space for reflection and truth.

> **The companion book (optional)** — for deeper context, teaching, and reflection alongside the weekly journal work.
>
> **A pen or pencil** — choose one that writes smoothly and feels good in your hand.
>
> **A quiet space** — even a small corner where you can breathe and think without interruption.
>
> **A Bible or Scripture app** (optional) — for deeper reflection on the weekly verse.
>
> **Colored pencils or markers** — for the weekly coloring page.
>
> **A bookmark or sticky notes** — to mark pages you want to revisit.
>
> **A glass of water or warm tea** — to support grounding while you write.

Emotional & Mental Preparation

These inner tools matter just as much—sometimes more—than the practical ones.

> ✔ **Honesty**
>
>> Bring the real you.
>>
>> Not the polished version.
>>
>> Not the "strong" version.
>>
>> Just the true one.

You don't have to write beautifully—you only need to write truthfully.

✔ Self-Compassion

> Your identity story may touch tender places.
>
> Hold yourself gently.

You are not behind. You are not late. You are simply arriving.

✔ Curiosity

> Curiosity opens doors that judgment keeps closed.

Instead of asking "Why am I like this?" try "I wonder what this is trying to tell me."

✔ Permission to Feel

> Some weeks will feel light. Others may stir deeper things.
>
> Let your emotions be welcome guests—not intruders.

You don't have to fix anything. You're just noticing.

✔ A Non-Rushed Pace

> Take as long as your heart needs.
>
> Some questions may take minutes.
>
> Others may take days.

Healing has its own rhythm.

✔ Willingness to Let Go of Old Stories

> Each week invites you to release something that no longer serves you.
>
> You don't have to feel ready.

Just be willing.

✓ A Body-Centered Mindset

> Noticing where you feel tension or openness in your body helps you recognize truth more clearly.

Your body is an ally on this journey.

✓ Grace

> For the days you forget.
>
> For the days you avoid.
>
> For the days you feel stuck.
>
> For the identity you are learning to leave behind.
>
> For the versions of yourself you needed in order to survive.
>
> For the people who assigned you names, roles, or worth that you never asked for.
>
> For the parts of your story that still ache as they unravel.
>
> For the truth you are growing into, one breath at a time.

Grace is the soft space between who you were, who others said you had to be, and who you are becoming now.

This journey is not about perfection—it's about presence.

Optional Supports

Soft music

Essential oils

A cozy blanket

A candle or gentle light

Your favorite drink

A grounding object (stone, cross, leaf, anything meaningful)

These are not required, but they can help create a sense of emotional safety and comfort.

You don't need much—just you.

Show up as you are.

    Be honest.

    Be tender.

    Be willing to grow.

This journal will meet you where you are and walk with you as you rise into your truth, identity, and worth.

Overview of the RISE™ Framework

A Pathway Back to Whole-Being Wellness

RISE is more than a wellness model — it is an invitation back to the way you were created to live:

Rooted, Intentional, Strong, and Energized.

When people rise, they rise in four dimensions — body, mind, spirit, and community — each supporting the other like threads in a tapestry of wholeness.

The **Identity & Worth** volume helps you begin this journey by grounding you in who you are, before expanding into deeper lifestyle patterns in future volumes.

RISE provides language, symbols, and simple practices that you can begin to weave into your daily life one small shift at a time.

Below is the complete framework.

R — Rooted

Rooted people are steady, grounded, nourished, and connected.

Labels, storms, or circumstances do not define them, because their identity is anchored in something deeper and more eternal.

> Being rooted means:
>
>> Strong internal foundations
>>
>> Eating what nourishes
>>
>> Slowing down enough to listen
>>
>> Living from truth, not reaction
>>
>> Returning to who you are beneath old labels

Rootedness gives people stability and resilience so they can grow without fear of being uprooted.

I — Intentional

Intentional living means moving through the world with clarity, purpose, and conscious choice.

It is the opposite of living on autopilot or from inherited beliefs.

> Intentionality expresses itself as:

Mindfulness

Choosing rather than drifting

Creating rhythms instead of reacting

Speaking truth with compassion

Aligning actions with values

Intentional people move with meaning, even in small decisions.

S — Strong

Strength is not force — it is integrity, emotional stability, and inner resilience.

It is the ability to stay centered in truth even when circumstances shake.

This dimension includes:

Emotional strength

Boundaries

Courage

Resilience

Balanced confidence

Willingness to grow

Strength allows people to face life with steady hearts and a grounded identity.

E — Energized

Energized living is not frantic hyper-productivity — it is sustainable, life-giving vitality.

It is the natural result of alignment, nourishment, and inner freedom.

Energized people experience:

Joy that flows without force

Healthy rhythms of work and rest

Clarity instead of exhaustion

Purpose without burnout

A sense of internal lightness

This is what it means to be fully alive.

The Circle of Wholeness Model

A Whole-System View of Human Flourishing

The Circle of Wholeness is the visual framework that holds the entire RISE model.

It teaches that wellness is not linear — it is circular, interconnected, and dynamic.

Every area of life impacts every other.

Small choices ripple outward.

Minor shifts create significant healing.

You cannot "fix" one area without touching the whole.

The Circle of Wholeness comprises 9 Pillars, each represented by a simple symbol.

Each symbol reflects a layer of wellness and a daily practice that keeps the whole system thriving.

These symbols are intentionally universal, spiritual, and nature-based, so you can connect with them in your own way.

The next page gives you a simple overview of the nine-pillar ecosystem.

The Nine Pillars of Wholeness

The pillars are listed in order. Each includes:

Symbol

Meaning

Daily practice focus

Reflection question

1. The Tree of Life — Rooted Health

Meaning: Connection, nourishment, vitality.

Wholeness begins underground: strong roots create strong lives.

Practice:

Eat from creation (living foods)

Move daily with gratitude

Rest before exhaustion

Reflection:

What keeps my roots strong today?

2. The Scales of Balance — Living in Alignment

Meaning: Harmony across body, mind, spirit, and relationships.

Balance is alignment, not perfection.

Practice:

Pause mid-day to breathe and recenter

Simplify one crowded area

Reflection:

Where can I recalibrate gently instead of striving?

3. The Radiant Human — Flowing Energy Within

Meaning: Inner light and vitality flow freely when beliefs, thoughts, and spirit agree.

Practice:

Begin with three deep breaths

Practice prayer, meditation, or mindful movement

Reflection:

How can I let my inner light guide my pace?

4. Hands of Stewardship — Nurturing What's Given

Meaning: Responsibility, gratitude, and tending what has been entrusted.

Practice:

Do one act of care for your body, home, or relationships

Give encouragement or gratitude

Reflection:

What am I stewarding with love today?

5. The Garden Path — Healing as a Journey

Meaning: Growth is not linear. Real healing bends, curves, and unfolds over time.

Practice:

    Notice progress without judgment

    Rest purposefully once a week

Reflection:

    What is today teaching me about patience?

6. The Water Ripple — The Power of Small Choices

Meaning: Every choice sends ripples into the whole system.

Practice:

    Do one nourishing action

    Notice its ripple through mood and relationships

Reflection:

    How can one small shift bring wider peace?

7. The Circle of People — Healing Together

Meaning: Belonging and connection are essential. We heal in community, not isolation.

Practice:

> Reach out to encourage someone

> Ask for help when needed

Reflection:

> Who forms my circle of support?

8. Sunrise Over Mountains — Renewal & Hope

Meaning: Dawn after darkness; every day is a new beginning.

Practice:

> Begin with gratitude

> Reframe setbacks as sunrise lessons

Reflection:

> Where do I see new light emerging?

9. The Heart in Creation — Love as the Core of Wholeness

Meaning: Love sustains the ecosystem of wellness — compassion, unity, and divine rhythm.

Practice:

Speak kindness to yourself and others

Do one act of care for creation

Reflection:

How can I let love move through me today?

How the RISE Framework, Circle of Wholeness, and 9 Pillars Work Together

These three layers form a complete ecosystem:

RISE = the four qualities of a whole person

Rooted • Intentional • Strong • Energized

The Circle of Wholeness = the whole-life model

An interconnected system where every area influences the others.

The Nine Pillars = the daily practices

Simple, repeatable habits that bring real change over time.

Together, they help you:

Remember their worth

Strengthen your internal identity

Heal body, mind, and spirit

Reconnect with community

Establish nourishing rhythms

Develop emotional stability

Return to the Creator's design

Transform from within

Week 1

Identity & Worth
Why Labels Can Limit Your Life

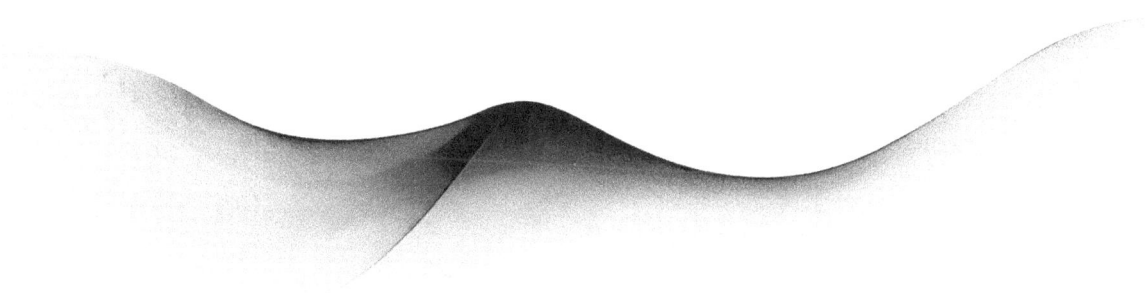

Labels shape us long before we realize it. Some were spoken over us. Some we absorbed quietly. Some were born from hurt or survival.

This week, you begin gently noticing the names you've carried — and remembering that identity can be renewed.

"You are not the names life stuck to you.
You are the one quietly growing beneath them. "

~ Angel Tate Keaton

What thoughts or emotions rise as you begin this week?

Awareness Check-in

What sensations do you notice in your chest, throat, shoulders, or stomach?

What emotion is closest to the surface right now?

What is one need your body or heart is expressing today?

Identity & Labels

What labels, spoken or unspoken, have I carried?

Which label stayed with me the longest?

Which labels came from family, culture, trauma, or past roles?

Which labels felt protective at one time but limits me now?

What label am I ready to release?

Diving Deeper

What choices, behaviors, or relationships in my life were shaped by a label I believed about myself?

....

....

....

....

When have I held back, stayed small, or silenced myself because of how I saw myself?

....

....

....

....

How does my sense of worth shift when I see myself as someone growing, healing, and becoming—not someone defined by old labels?

....

....

....

....

My Inner Dialog

Release & Replace

What label has limited your sense of worth?

HELLO
MY NAME IS

What is a truer, freer identity statement?

Identity Statements

Write 5 identity statements that reflect truth, not labels you've carried.

1.

2.

3.

4.

5.

Write 5 "I am becoming..." statements that reflect a freer sense of self-worth.

1.

2.

3.

4.

5.

Anchoring Truth
What truth matters most to carry forward?

Embodiment Practice

This Week's Identity Truth

_____
_____
_____
_____

What It Means To Me

_____
_____
_____
_____
_____

How I Will Practice It

How will I practice this truth in daily life?

_____
_____
_____
_____

What reminder will ground me in this truth?

_____
_____
_____
_____

What will help me return to this truth on difficult days?

_____
_____
_____
_____
_____
_____

End-of-Week Reflection

What shifted?

....
....
....
....

What felt hard?

....
....
....
....

What felt healing?

....
....
....
....

What surprised you?

....
....
....
....

What truth carried you?

....
....
....
....

What are you proud of yourself for?

....
....
....
....

Week 2

Comparison
The Thief of Contentment

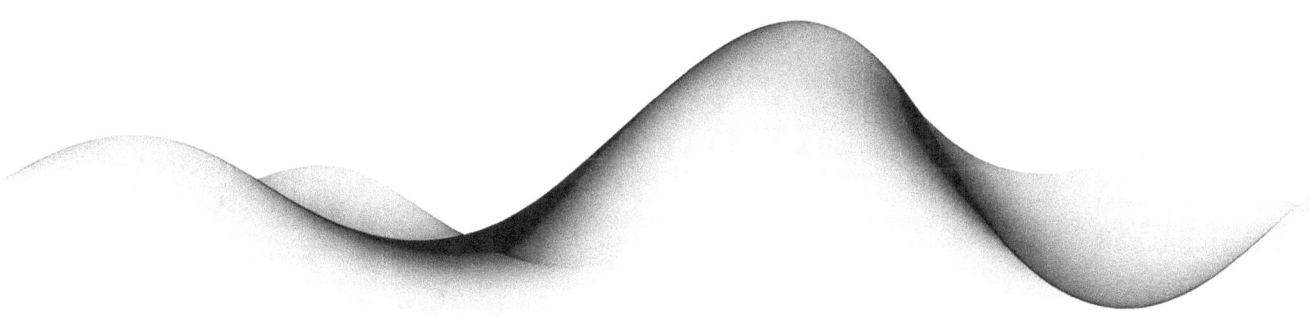

Comparison sneaks in quietly and convinces us that who we are and what we have is not enough.

This week invites you to reclaim peace by shifting your eyes from others' timelines back to your own rooted path.

"Comparison blinds us to the miracles happening in our own lane."
~ Unknown

What thoughts or emotions rise as you begin this week?

_____

_____

_____

_____

_____

_____

_____

Awareness Check-in

What sensations do you notice in your chest, throat, shoulders, or stomach?

What emotion is closest to the surface right now?

What is one need your body or heart is expressing today?

Comparison & Contentment

In what areas do I compare myself most often?

Whose standards am I measuring myself against?

How does comparison affect my confidence or peace?

What strengths of mine get overlooked when I compare?

What would contentment look like for me this week?

Diving Deeper

When did I first start comparing myself to others, and what was happening in my life at that time?

....

....

....

....

What emotions show up when I compare—envy, insecurity, shame, pressure, or fear—and what might those emotions be trying to tell me?

....

....

....

....

What truth can I return to when I feel "behind," and how does remembering my own path restore peace?

....

....

....

....

My Inner Dialog

Release & Replace

What comparison steals your peace?

HELLO
MY NAME IS

What is YOUR truth apart from comparison?

Identity Statements

Write 5 identity statements rooted in *your own lane*, not comparison.

1.

_____

_____

2.

_____

_____

3.

_____

_____

4.

_____

_____

5.

_____

_____

Write 5 "I am becoming..." statements that reflect contentment and self-trust.

1.

_____

_____

2.

_____

_____

3.

_____

_____

4.

_____

_____

5.

_____

_____

Anchoring Truth
What truth matters most to carry forward?

_____

_____

Embodiment Practice

This Week's Identity Truth

What It Means To Me

How I Will Practice It

How will I practice this truth in daily life?

What reminder will ground me in this truth?

What will help me return to this truth on difficult days?

End-of-Week Reflection

What shifted?

What felt hard?

What felt healing?

What surprised you?

What truth carried you?

What are you proud of yourself for?

Week 3

Voices
Whose Words Shape Your Worth?

The voices we absorb—family, culture, religion, and even our inner critic—can shape our identity in ways that don't honor who we truly are.

This week helps you sort through those influences and hold on only to what aligns with truth and wholeness.

*"Your voice is evidence that you matter.
Every time you speak truth,
you agree with your own value."*
~ Angel Tate Keaton

What thoughts or emotions rise as you begin this week?

_____

_____

_____

_____

_____

_____

Awareness Check-in

What sensations do you notice in your chest, throat, shoulders, or stomach?

What emotion is closest to the surface right now?

What is one need your body or heart is expressing today?

My Voice, My Value

When do I feel most heard and valued?

When have I silenced myself to keep peace or avoid conflict?

What messages taught me that my voice didn't matter?

What truth do I want to claim about my voice now?

What small moment this week can help me use my voice more freely?

Diving Deeper

Where in my life did I first learn to quiet my voice, and how did that shape the way I show up today?

....

....

....

....

How has staying silent affected my relationships, confidence, or sense of self over time?

....

....

....

....

What would it look like to honor my voice with compassion and courage, even in small everyday moments?

....

....

....

....

My Inner Dialog

Release & Replace

What silencing message or false belief does not belong to you?

HELLO
MY NAME IS

What truth amplifies your voice?

Identity Statements

Write 5 identity statements that honor your voice, needs, and value.

1.

_____

2.

_____

3.

_____

4.

_____

5.

_____

Write 5 "I am becoming..." statements about speaking up with truth and confidence.

1.

_____

2.

_____

3.

_____

4.

_____

5.

_____

Anchoring Truth
What truth matters most to carry forward?

_____

Embodiment Practice

This Week's Identity Truth

What It Means To Me

How I Will Practice It

How will I practice this truth in daily life?

What reminder will ground me in this truth?

What will help me return to this truth on difficult days?

End-of-Week Reflection

What shifted?

. . . .
. . . .
. . . .
. . . .
. . . .

What felt hard?

. . . .
. . . .
. . . .
. . . .
. . . .

What felt healing?

. . . .
. . . .
. . . .
. . . .
. . . .

What surprised you?

. . . .
. . . .
. . . .
. . . .
. . . .

What truth carried you?

. . . .
. . . .
. . . .
. . . .

What are you proud of yourself for?

. . . .
. . . .
. . . .
. . . .

Week 4

Shame vs. Conviction
Learning the Difference

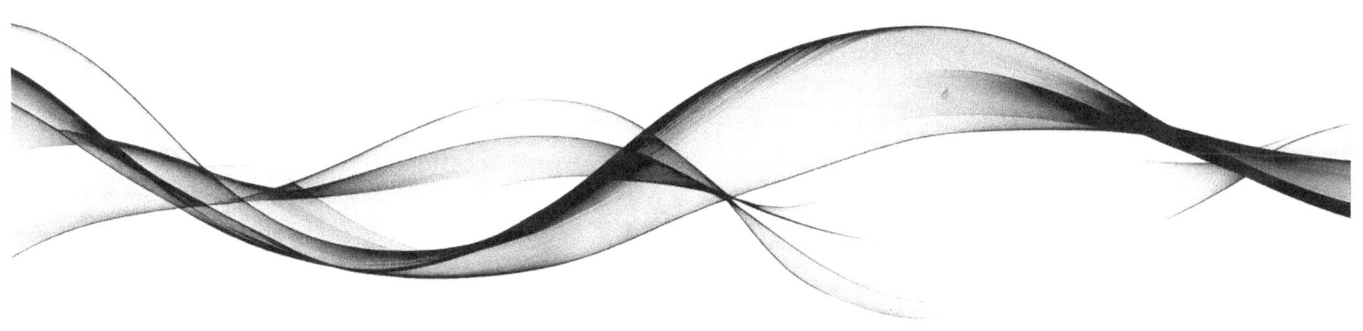

Shame tells you who you are is flawed, while guilt simply reveals where you've gone off course.

This week uncovers that difference so you can release shame's grip and return to compassionate self-alignment.

"Shame says 'this is who you are.'
Truth says 'this is what happened—
is not who you are.'"
~ Unknown

What thoughts or emotions rise as you begin this week?

_____

_____

_____

_____

_____

_____

Awareness Check-in

What sensations do you notice in your chest, throat, shoulders, or stomach?

What emotion is closest to the surface right now?

What is one need your body or heart is expressing today?

Shame & the Self

What moments or messages have shaped how I see myself?

Where do I still feel "not enough," even if I know it isn't true?

What part of my identity does shame try to attach itself to?

What is actually true about me beneath that shame?

What does freedom from shame look like for me this week?

Diving Deeper

When did I first start believing something was "wrong" with me, and whose voice or moment does that belief trace back to?

....

....

....

....

How has shame shaped the way I speak to myself, show up in relationships, or protect myself from being seen?

....

....

....

....

What would it feel like to respond to myself with compassion instead of criticism when shame rises?

....

....

....

....

My Inner Dialog

Release & Replace

What shame-based belief does not belong to you?

HELLO
MY NAME IS

What identity truth sets you free?

Identity Statements

Write 5 identity statements that separate who you are from what shame has told you.

1.
_____

_____

2.
_____

_____

3.
_____

_____

4.
_____

_____

5.
_____

_____

Write 5 "I am becoming..." statements that reflect the freedom of being seen without shame.

1.
_____

_____

2.
_____

_____

3.
_____

_____

4.
_____

_____

5.
_____

_____

Anchoring Truth
What truth matters most to carry forward?

_____

_____

Embodiment Practice

This Week's Identity Truth

What It Means To Me

How I Will Practice It

How will I practice this truth in daily life?

What reminder will ground me in this truth?

What will help me return to this truth on difficult days?

End-of-Week Reflection

What shifted?

. . . .
. . . .
. . . .
. . . .

What felt hard?

. . . .
. . . .
. . . .
. . . .

What felt healing?

. . . .
. . . .
. . . .
. . . .

What surprised you?

. . . .
. . . .
. . . .
. . . .

What truth carried you?

. . . .
. . . .
. . . .
. . . .

What are you proud of yourself for?

. . . .
. . . .
. . . .
. . . .

Week 5

The Stories We Tell Ourselves
Rewriting Internal Narratives

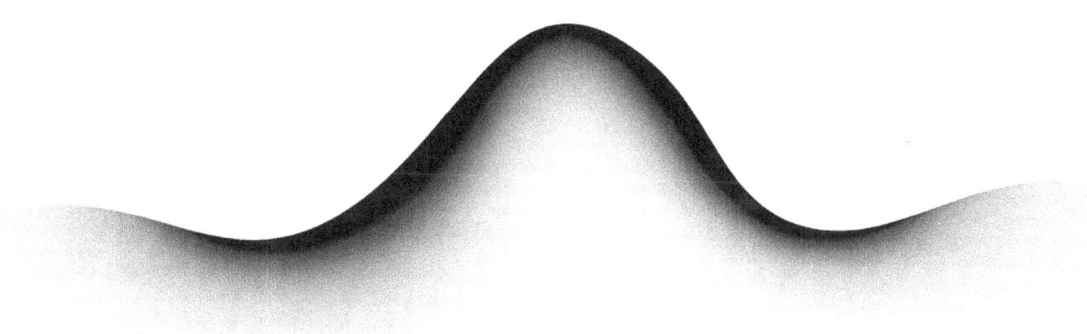

We often live inside narratives formed long before we had the power to question them.

This week empowers you to rewrite the stories that no longer serve your healing or identity.

"When you change the story you tell yourself, you change the future you are walking toward."
~ Angel Tate Keaton

What thoughts or emotions rise as you begin this week?

_____

_____

_____

_____

_____

_____

Awareness Check-in

What sensations do you notice in your chest, throat, shoulders, or stomach?

What emotion is closest to the surface right now?

What is one need your body or heart is expressing today?

The Stories I Tell Myself

What is a story I've told myself for a long time?

Who or what originally influenced this story?

How has this story protected me or limited me?

What evidence challenges the story I've believed?

What new narrative feels truer and healthier?

Diving Deeper

What emotions come up when I think about letting go of this old story—and what might those emotions be trying to protect?

....

....

....

....

How has this story shaped the way I see myself, my worth, or what I believe is possible for me?

....

....

....

....

If I spoke to myself with compassion and truth, how would I rewrite this story in a way that supports my growth?

....

....

....

....

My Inner Dialog

Release & Replace

What old story or narrative is no longer true?

HELLO
MY NAME IS

What new story do you choose to tell?

Identity Statements

Write 5 identity statements that reflect truth, not old survival narratives.

1.

_____

_____

2.

_____

_____

3.

_____

_____

4.

_____

_____

5.

_____

_____

Write 5 "I am becoming..." statements that reflect the story you want to live going forward.

1.

_____

_____

2.

_____

_____

3.

_____

_____

4.

_____

_____

5.

_____

_____

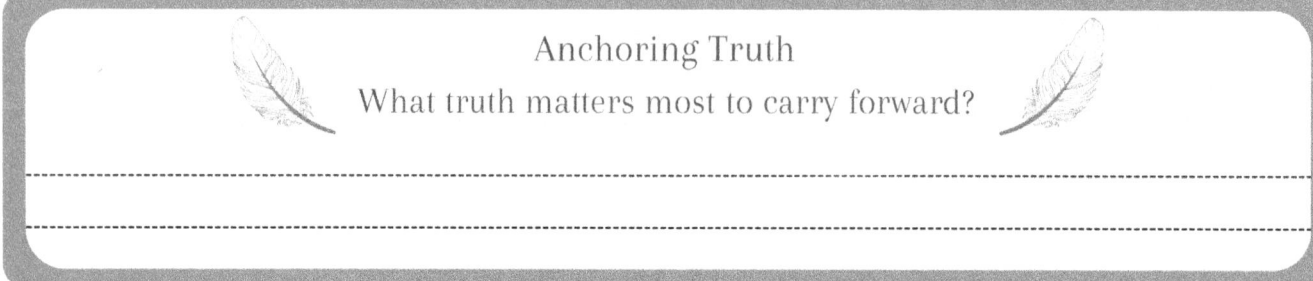

Anchoring Truth
What truth matters most to carry forward?

_____

_____

Embodiment Practice

This Week's Identity Truth

_____
_____
_____

What It Means To Me

_____
_____
_____
_____

How I Will Practice It

How will I practice this truth in daily life?

_____
_____
_____
_____

What reminder will ground me in this truth?

_____
_____
_____
_____

What will help me return to this truth on difficult days?

_____
_____
_____
_____
_____

End-of-Week Reflection

What shifted?

. . . .
. . . .
. . . .
. . . .

What felt hard?

. . . .
. . . .
. . . .
. . . .

What felt healing?

. . . .
. . . .
. . . .
. . . .

What surprised you?

. . . .
. . . .
. . . .
. . . .

What truth carried you?

. . . .
. . . .
. . . .
. . . .

What are you proud of yourself for?

. . . .
. . . .
. . . .
. . . .

Week 6

Resilience
Bouncing Back
Without Losing Yourself

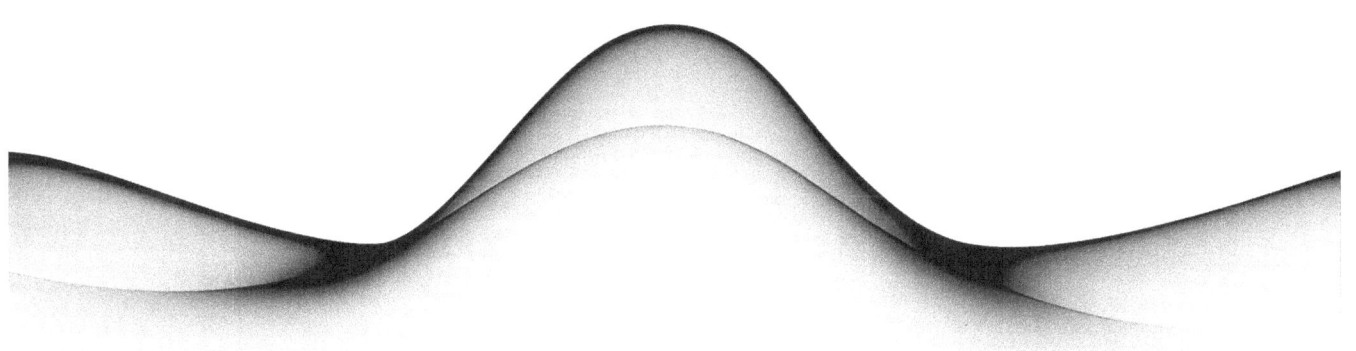

True resilience isn't about toughness—it's about staying connected to your core when life shakes you.

This week strengthens your ability to rise without abandoning your authenticity.

"Resilience is not becoming harder.
It is learning how to rise
without abandoning who you are."
~ Unknown

What thoughts or emotions rise as you begin this week?

_____

_____

_____

_____

_____

_____

_____

Awareness Check-in

What sensations do you notice in your chest, throat, shoulders, or stomach?

What emotion is closest to the surface right now?

What is one need your body or heart is expressing today?

Resilience Without Losing Myself

What part of me feels tired or stretched thin?

What has helped me bounce back in the past?

What signs show me I'm beginning to feel overwhelmed?

Where do I need gentleness instead of toughness this week?

What would it look like to be resilient and deeply myself?

Diving Deeper

Where have I learned to push past my limits, and how has that shaped the way I define "strength"?

....

....

....

....

What part of me is asking to slow down, rest, or be cared for—and what makes it hard to honor that need?

....

....

....

....

How can I practice resilience that honors my humanity instead of requiring me to abandon myself?

....

....

....

....

My Inner Dialog

Release & Replace

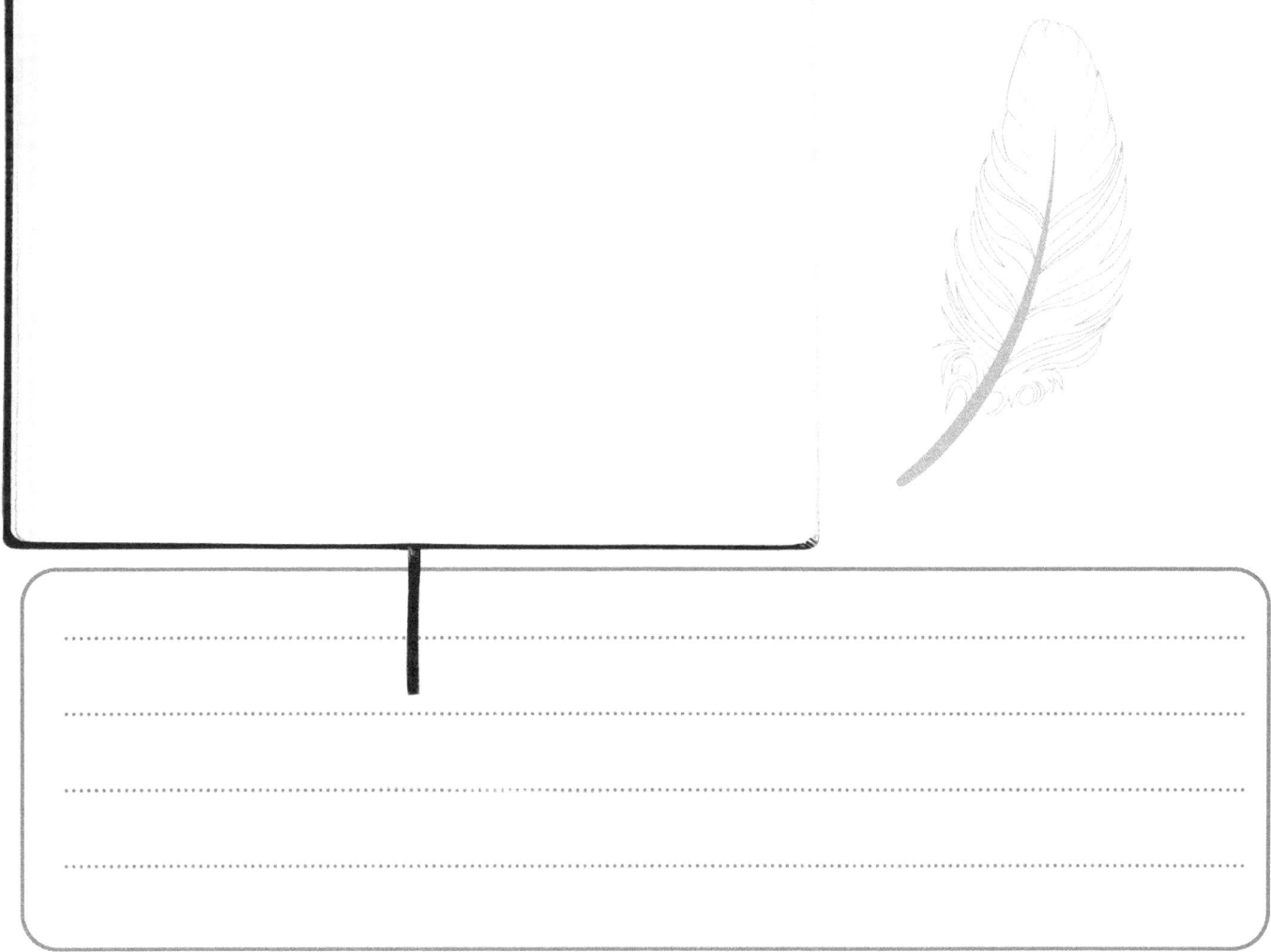

What belief makes you feel weak or fragile?

HELLO
MY NAME IS

What truth strengthens your resilience?

Identity Statements

Write 5 identity statements that honor your strength and your softness.

1.

2.

3.

4.

5.

Write 5 "I am becoming..." statements that reflect grounded resilience.

1.

2.

3.

4.

5.

Anchoring Truth
What truth matters most to carry forward?

Embodiment Practice

This Week's Identity Truth

What It Means To Me

How I Will Practice It

How will I practice this truth in daily life?

What reminder will ground me in this truth?

What will help me return to this truth on difficult days?

End-of-Week Reflection

What shifted?

What felt hard?

What felt healing?

What surprised you?

What truth carried you?

What are you proud of yourself for?

Week 7

Authenticity
Removing the Masks

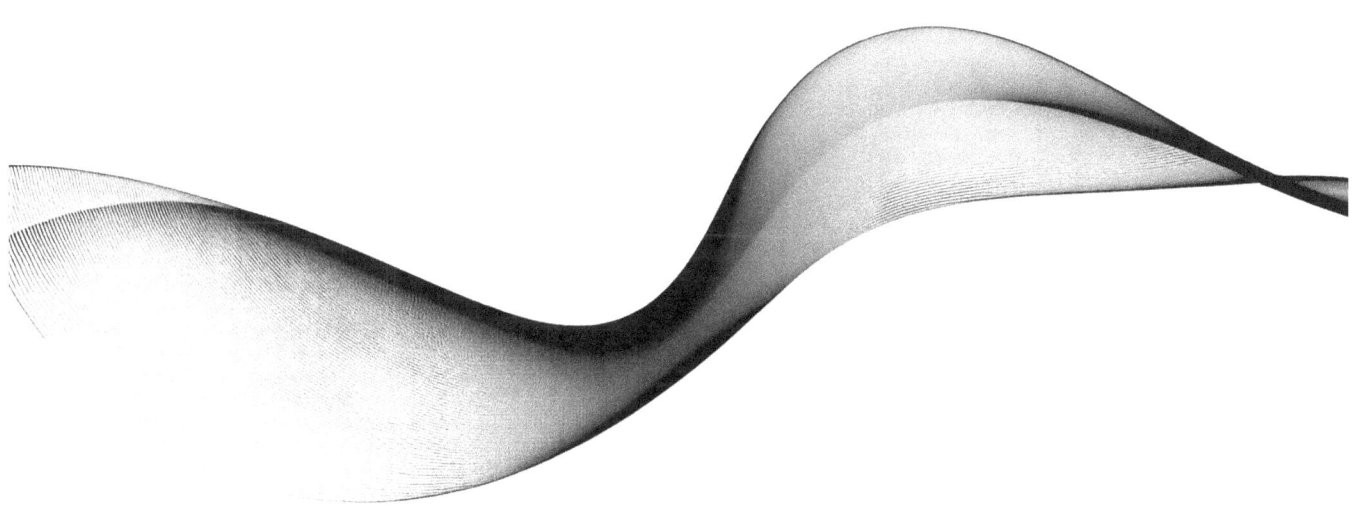

The masks we wear may keep us safe, but they also keep us small.

This week gently guides you toward showing up as your full, unhidden self.

*"Every mask you lay down
makes more room for
your real face to shine through."*
~ Angel Tate Keaton

What thoughts or emotions rise as you begin this week?

_____

_____

_____

_____

_____

_____

Awareness Check-in

What sensations do you notice in your chest, throat, shoulders, or stomach?

What emotion is closest to the surface right now?

What is one need your body or heart is expressing today?

Living Without the Mask

What mask or persona do I slip into most often?

What parts of me feel safest to reveal?

What parts still feel guarded or hidden?

What relationship feels safest for me to show up authentically?

What is one small step toward being more fully myself?

Diving Deeper

What fear or past experience makes wearing a "mask" feel safer than being fully seen?

....

....

....

....

How does hiding parts of myself impact my relationships, confidence, or sense of belonging?

....

....

....

....

What would it feel like to trust that my authentic self is worthy of being known, even if not everyone understands me?

....

....

....

....

My Inner Dialog

Release & Replace

What mask or role hides the real you?

HELLO
MY NAME IS

What truth brings you closer to authenticity?

Identity Statements

Write 5 identity statements that reflect your true self, not the roles or masks you've worn.

1.

_____

_____

2.

_____

_____

3.

_____

_____

4.

_____

_____

5.

_____

_____

Write 5 "I am becoming..." statements that reflect showing up as your whole, honest self.

1.

_____

_____

2.

_____

_____

3.

_____

_____

4.

_____

_____

5.

_____

_____

Anchoring Truth
What truth matters most to carry forward?

_____

_____

Embodiment Practice

This Week's Identity Truth

What It Means To Me

How I Will Practice It

How will I practice this truth in daily life?

What reminder will ground me in this truth?

What will help me return to this truth on difficult days?

End-of-Week Reflection

What shifted?

....
....
....
....

What felt hard?

....
....
....
....

What felt healing?

....
....
....
....

What surprised you?

....
....
....
....

What truth carried you?

....
....
....
....

What are you proud of yourself for?

....
....
....
....

Week 8

Identity in Transitions
When Roles Change

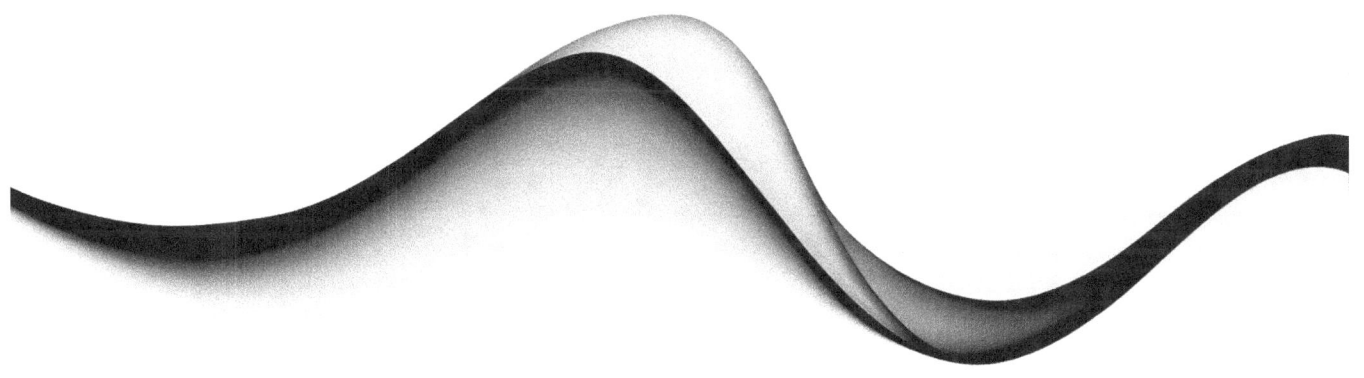

Life transitions—parenting, career shifts, aging, loss—can blur our sense of self.

This week helps you anchor your identity in who you are, not in the roles you perform.

*"When roles shift and seasons change,
your truest identity is still held
in the One who named you."*
~ Faith Reflection

What thoughts or emotions rise as you begin this week?

_____

_____

_____

_____

_____

_____

Awareness Check-in

What sensations do you notice in your chest, throat, shoulders, or stomach?

What emotion is closest to the surface right now?

What is one need your body or heart is expressing today?

Identity in Transitions

What role or season am I transitioning out of?

What identity was attached to that role?

What fears come up as this chapter shifts?

What strengths am I bringing with me into this new season?

Who am I becoming through this transition?

Diving Deeper

What beliefs about myself are being challenged or reshaped in this transition—and what does that reveal about my growth?

....

....

....

....

Which parts of me feel hesitant to let go of the old season, and what do those parts need—reassurance, closure, or permission?

....

....

....

....

How might this transition create space for a truer, healthier, or more aligned version of me to emerge?

....

....

....

....

My Inner Dialog

Release & Replace

What role-based identity no longer fits?

HELLO
MY NAME IS

What identity truth remains constant?

Identity Statements

Write 5 identity statements reflect you, not the roles you play.

1.
_____

2.
_____

3.
_____

4.
_____

5.
_____

Write 5 "I am becoming..." statements that reflect who you're growing into during this transition.

1.
_____

2.
_____

3.
_____

4.
_____

5.
_____

Anchoring Truth
What truth matters most to carry forward?

_____
_____

Embodiment Practice

This Week's Identity Truth

What It Means To Me

How I Will Practice It

How will I practice this truth in daily life?

What reminder will ground me in this truth?

What will help me return to this truth on difficult days?

End-of-Week Reflection

What shifted?

What felt hard?

What felt healing?

What surprised you?

What truth carried you?

What are you proud of yourself for?

120

Week 9

Faith & Worth
Rooting Identity in Being Beloved

Worth isn't earned; it's received from the One who formed you with intention.

This week explores how seeing yourself as beloved reshapes confidence, peace, and purpose.

"Worth is not earned;
it is received.
You are beloved
long before you
perform, achieve, or prove."
~ Angel Tate Keaton

What thoughts or emotions rise as you begin this week?

_____

_____

_____

_____

_____

_____

_____

Awareness Check-in

What sensations do you notice in your chest, throat, shoulders, or stomach?

What emotion is closest to the surface right now?

What is one need your body or heart is expressing today?

Beloved Identity

What do I believe YHVH says about my worth?

What belief about myself is hardest to reconcile with being "beloved"?

Where have I confused performance with identity?

What brings me back to divine love when I forget who I am?

What truth about being beloved do I want to root into this week?

Diving Deeper

Where did I first learn to question my worth, and how is that belief different from what YHVH says about me?

....

....

....

....

How has striving, people-pleasing, or performing shaped the way I see myself—and what does my soul feel like when I stop striving?

....

....

....

....

If I fully believed I was beloved, how would I speak to myself, care for myself, and move through the world this week?

....

....

....

....

My Inner Dialog

Release & Replace

What belief about your worth conflicts with being beloved by the Father?

HELLO
MY NAME IS

What does the Father say about you?

Identity Statements

Write 5 identity statements grounded in being seen, known, and beloved.

1.

_____

_____

2.

_____

_____

3.

_____

_____

4.

_____

_____

5.

_____

_____

Write 5 "I am becoming..." statements that reflect living from belovedness.

1.

_____

_____

2.

_____

_____

3.

_____

_____

4.

_____

_____

5.

_____

_____

Anchoring Truth
What truth matters most to carry forward?

_____

_____

Embodiment Practice

This Week's Identity Truth

_____
_____
_____

What It Means To Me

_____
_____
_____

How I Will Practice It

How will I practice this truth in daily life?

_____
_____
_____
_____

What reminder will ground me in this truth?

_____
_____
_____
_____

What will help me return to this truth on difficult days?

_____
_____
_____
_____
_____

End-of-Week Reflection

What shifted?

....
....
....
....

What felt hard?

....
....
....
....

What felt healing?

....
....
....
....

What surprised you?

....
....
....
....

What truth carried you?

....
....
....
....

What are you proud of yourself for?

....
....
....
....

Week 10

Body Image & Self-Talk
Shifting from Criticism to Compassion

The way you speak to your body becomes the way you live in it.

This week invites you into kinder internal conversations that cultivate compassion instead of criticism.

"Your body is not an enemy to conquer;
it is a faithful witness
asking to be treated with kindness."
~ Unknown

What thoughts or emotions rise as you begin this week?

_____

_____

_____

_____

_____

_____

Awareness Check-in

What sensations do you notice in your chest, throat, shoulders, or stomach?

What emotion is closest to the surface right now?

What is one need your body or heart is expressing today?

Compassion Toward My Body

What messages shaped how I view my body?

What part of my body receives the harshest self-talk?

What has my body carried me through that deserves gratitude?

What compassionate truth can replace my critical thoughts?

How can I speak to myself with kindness this week?

Diving Deeper

Where did I learn to be at odds with my body, and what would it look like to offer that part of me understanding instead of judgment?

....

....

....

....

How has my body tried to communicate its needs—through tension, fatigue, cravings, or emotions—and how well have I listened?

....

....

....

....

What would change in my daily life if I treated my body as a partner rather than a project to fix?

....

....

....

....

My Inner Dialog

Release & Replace

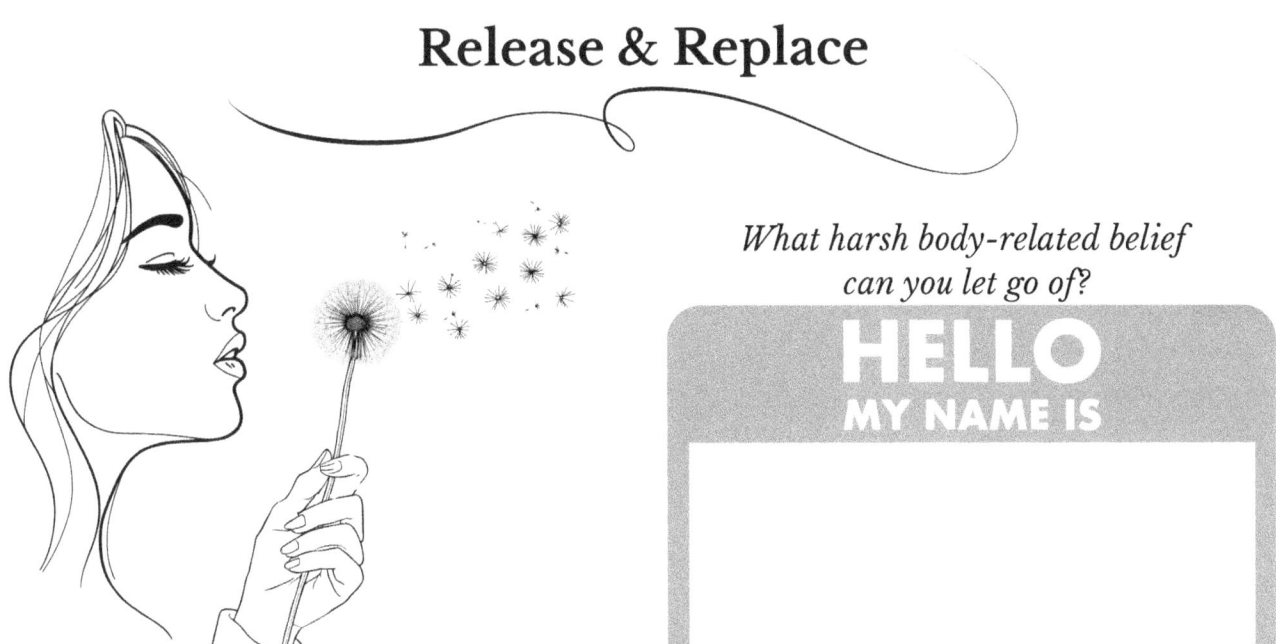

What harsh body-related belief can you let go of?

HELLO
MY NAME IS

What compassionate truth replaces it?

Identity Statements

Write 5 identity statements that honor your body and speak kindness over it.

1.

2.

3.

4.

5.

Write 5 "I am becoming..." statements that reflect compassionate self-talk.

1.

2.

3.

4.

5.

Anchoring Truth
What truth matters most to carry forward?

Embodiment Practice

This Week's Identity Truth

_____
_____
_____
_____

What It Means To Me

_____
_____
_____
_____

How I Will Practice It

How will I practice this truth in daily life?

_____
_____
_____
_____

What reminder will ground me in this truth?

_____
_____
_____
_____

What will help me return to this truth on difficult days?

_____
_____
_____
_____
_____

End-of-Week Reflection

What shifted?

....
....
....
....

What felt hard?

....
....
....
....

What felt healing?

....
....
....
....

What surprised you?

....
....
....
....

What truth carried you?

....
....
....
....

What are you proud of yourself for?

....
....
....
....

Week 11

Failure as Teacher, Not Title
Reframing Mistakes as Growth

Failure is not a label—it's a lesson wrapped in experience.

This week reframes mistakes as opportunities for growth, courage, and clarity.

"Failure is a moment,
not a name tag.
Let it teach you,
not define you. "
~ Angel Tate Keaton

What thoughts or emotions rise as you begin this week?

_____

_____

_____

_____

_____

_____

Awareness Check-in

What sensations do you notice in your chest, throat, shoulders, or stomach?

What emotion is closest to the surface right now?

What is one need your body or heart is expressing today?

Growing Through Setbacks

What recent mistake or setback still lingers in my mind?

What meaning did I attach to that moment?

What did that experience reveal about my strengths or needs?

What truth reminds me that failure is not my identity?

What growth am I willing to embrace moving forward?

Diving Deeper

What story do I tell myself when I fail, and where did that story originally come from?

....

....

....

....

How have past setbacks shaped my resilience, wisdom, or empathy in ways I often overlook?

....

....

....

....

If I saw this setback as a teacher instead of a verdict, what lesson might it be offering me right now?

....

....

....

....

My Inner Dialog

Release & Replace

What failure-based identity are you releasing?

HELLO
MY NAME IS

What growth-based truth can replace it?

Identity Statements

Write 5 identity statements that separate your identity from your mistakes.

1.

_____

2.

_____

3.

_____

4.

_____

5.

_____

Write 5 "I am becoming..." statements that reflect growth without shame.

1.

_____

2.

_____

3.

_____

4.

_____

5.

_____

Anchoring Truth
What truth matters most to carry forward?

_____

Embodiment Practice

This Week's Identity Truth

What It Means To Me

How I Will Practice It

How will I practice this truth in daily life?

What reminder will ground me in this truth?

What will help me return to this truth on difficult days?

End-of-Week Reflection

What shifted?

What felt hard?

What felt healing?

What surprised you?

What truth carried you?

What are you proud of yourself for?

Week 12

Community & Reflection
Seeing Yourself Through Healthy Connections

Healing deepens when it is shared, witnessed, and practiced in safe relationships.

This week helps you see yourself more clearly through connection, accountability, and mutual support.

*"Healing deepens
when we are seen with kindness.
Safe community
holds up a mirror of truth and grace."*
~ Unknown

What thoughts or emotions rise as you begin this week?

_____

_____

_____

_____

_____

_____

Awareness Check-in

What sensations do you notice in your chest, throat, shoulders, or stomach?

What emotion is closest to the surface right now?

What is one need your body or heart is expressing today?

Connection & Belonging

Who in my life helps me show up as my true self?

Where do I still feel unseen or misunderstood?

What has community taught me about my worth?

What connection felt healing or meaningful this week?

What kind of community am I becoming ready for?

Diving Deeper

How have past relationships shaped what I believe I deserve in connection—and which of those beliefs am I ready to release?

....

....

....

....

What parts of me feel most hungry for safe, authentic connection right now?

....

....

....

....

What would it look like to show up in community as someone who knows they are worthy of being seen and valued?

....

....

....

....

My Inner Dialog

Release & Replace

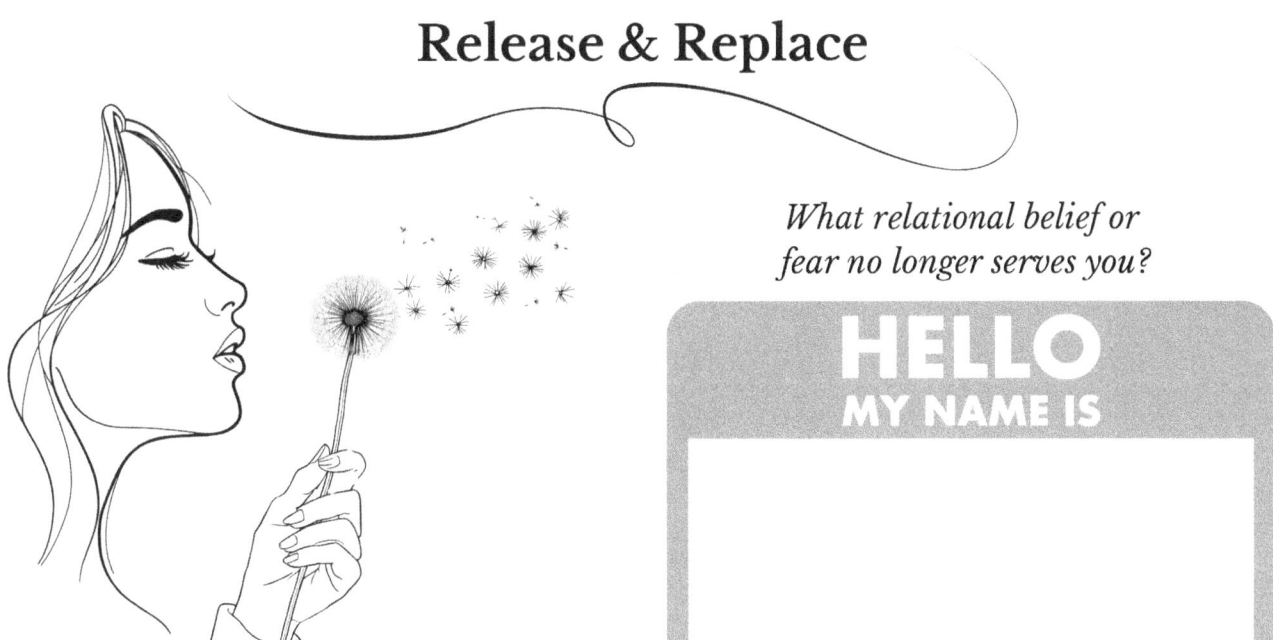

What relational belief or fear no longer serves you?

HELLO
MY NAME IS

What truth builds healthy connections?

Identity Statements

Write 5 identity statements shaped by connection, support, and truth-speaking community.

1.

_____

_____

_____

2.

_____

_____

3.

_____

_____

4.

_____

_____

5.

_____

_____

Write 5 "I am becoming..." statements that reflect how healthy community helps you grow.

1.

_____

_____

2.

_____

_____

3.

_____

_____

4.

_____

_____

5.

_____

_____

Anchoring Truth
What truth matters most to carry forward?

_____

_____

Embodiment Practice

This Week's Identity Truth

_____
_____
_____
_____

What It Means To Me

_____
_____
_____
_____

How I Will Practice It

How will I practice this truth in daily life?

_____
_____
_____
_____

What reminder will ground me in this truth?

_____
_____
_____
_____

What will help me return to this truth on difficult days?

_____
_____
_____
_____
_____

End-of-Week Reflection

What shifted?

. . . .
. . . .
. . . .
. . . .

What felt hard?

. . . .
. . . .
. . . .
. . . .

What felt healing?

. . . .
. . . .
. . . .
. . . .

What surprised you?

. . . .
. . . .
. . . .
. . . .

What truth carried you?

. . . .
. . . .
. . . .
. . . .

What are you proud of yourself for?

. . . .
. . . .
. . . .
. . . .

Final Reflections

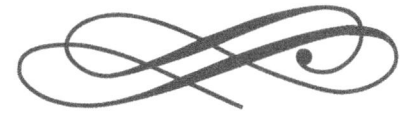

How has my sense of worth changed?

What truth feels most rooted now?

What will I carry forward?

How has my self-talk softened or strengthened?

My Identity Statement

Your Identity Statement

This is where you gather everything you've discovered over the last 12 weeks—your truth, your healing, your worth, your voice, and your becoming. Your Identity Statement is a long-form expression of who you are without the labels, masks, stories, or shame that once shaped you. Write freely. Write honestly. Write as if no one will ever read these words but you and your Creator.

How to Write It

- Reflect on your growth: Look back through the journal prompts and notice themes, truths, and breakthroughs.
- Name what is true: Write statements about your worth, your belonging, your identity, and the strengths you've uncovered.
- Release old narratives: Acknowledge what you are no longer carrying—old labels, limiting stories, or beliefs that no longer fit.
- Declare your becoming: Speak to the identity you are growing into—rooted, intentional, strong, and energized.

My Identity

My Identity Statement "RISE Style"

Your Identity Statement

After you complete your long-form Identity Statement, rewrite it using the RISE framework:

- R — Rooted: What truths are non-negotiable for you now?
- I — Intentional: How will you walk in your identity on purpose?
- S — Strong: What strengths or healed places are now part of who you are?
- E — Energized: What brings life, joy, or alignment to your identity moving forward?

This shorter RISE-style version becomes a daily or weekly declaration—a distilled version of the truth you want to carry with you.

Rooted

....
....
....
....

Intentional

....
....
....
....

Strong

....
....
....

Energized

....
....
....

Notes

Notes

Notes

Thank You

Thank you for choosing to enter this journey of identity, healing, and truth. Every page you've completed has been more than a reflection—it has been an act of courage. With each word you've written, you've taken another step toward wholeness, another step toward becoming Rooted in truth, Intentional in growth, Strong in spirit, and Energized in purpose.

Your presence in these pages matters. The insights you've uncovered, the stories you've released, and the truths you've reclaimed are sacred work. These are not small shifts—they are seeds of restoration, planted with honesty and tended with hope. You have shown up for yourself in a way that ripples into every corner of your life.

As you close this journal, may you continue to RISE—daily, gently, boldly. Carry this identity into your relationships, your choices, your rhythms, and your walk with the Creator. And remember: you are never walking alone. You are part of a larger story of redemption and renewal, and the Father delights to guide you, steady you, and speak truth over you.

Thank you for letting me walk a portion of this journey with you.

With gratitude and blessing,

Angel

Healthy in Heart Media, LLC

About R.I.S.E.

R.I.S.E. was created as a place of encouragement, clarity, and support for those choosing a whole food plant-based lifestyle and seeking to live in whole-being wellness. It is a framework for living that honors the Creator's original design for the body, mind, and spirit.

R.I.S.E. means:

Rooted in Truth – grounded in unshakable principles rather than passing trends.

Intentional in Habits – choosing daily practices that nourish and strengthen both body and soul.

Strong in Spirit – cultivating inner resilience, emotional stability, and faith for life's challenges.

Energized for Life – experiencing vibrancy, joy, and well-being through alignment, simplicity, and purpose.

Through R.I.S.E., you'll discover tools, teachings, and community support that help you walk toward wholeness with confidence. It's not only about food—it's about restoring balance, reclaiming identity, living with intention, and stepping into the fullness of life you were created for.

Every resource connected to R.I.S.E., including this journal, is designed to equip, uplift, and inspire you as you grow in wellness and walk out your calling with clarity and courage.

Feel free to reach out anytime to learn more about R.I.S.E. using the QR code below.

About the Author

Angel Tate Keaton is the founder of Healthy in Heart Media and the creator of the RISE™ Rooted, Intentional, Strong, Energized, a Whole-Being Wellness Framework. As a trauma survivor, teacher, author, and guide, Angel writes from the intersections of faith, identity, emotional healing, and whole-being restoration. Her work invites others to remember who they are beneath the labels, lies, and lifetimes of survival—and to step into the truth of who they were created to become.

After decades of healing work, Angel discovered that transformation doesn't begin with performance, perfection, or self-improvement—it starts with identity. This journal reflects her heart: to help others move from wounded stories to whole stories, from exhaustion to alignment, and from fractured self-image to beloved self-understanding. Through simple prompts, gentle questions, and the RISE rhythm of weekly reflection, she guides readers into a deeper clarity with a grounded confidence.

Angel believes that every person carries divine worth and that healing unfolds not by running faster but by returning to truth. Her mission is to create resources that help individuals rebuild their identity, release shame, reclaim resilience, and rise with purpose—spiritually, emotionally, and physically. Through books, journals, guides, community circles, and teaching, she is dedicated to equipping others to live lives that are rooted in truth, intentional in purpose, strong in identity, and energized in spirit.

Angel lives in Virginia with her husband, Todd, and their daughter, where they continue to write, teach, and walk out whole-being living with a shared passion for helping others rediscover the path back to themselves—and back to the One who made them.

Mission of Healthy in Heart

Healthy in Heart Media, LLC exists to help people return to wholeness—body, mind, and spirit—through Hebraic truth, Eden-aligned living, and compassionate, practical tools.

We:

- Publish books, journals, devotionals, and children's resources that make spiritual formation simple and doable.
- Guide households into oil-free, whole-food, plant-based eating through meal plans, prep systems, and gentle re-entry guides.
- Cultivate Sabbath and seasonal practices that restore pace, presence, and peace.

Mission in one line:

To restore shalom in real lives through truth, tools, and tables—so homes and communities become a little piece of Eden.

Join the Healthy in Heart Community

Wholeness is not a journey we walk alone. If this devotional cookbook has nourished your body and strengthened your spirit, I invite you to stay connected with a community that is growing, learning, and returning to the Creator's design together.

Visit the Healthy in Heart Website

Find more books, journals, recipes, botanical resources, and tools for whole-being wellness.

Website: HealthyInHeart.com

Follow Along on Social Media

Receive weekly encouragement, recipe ideas, spiritual reflections, and behind-the-scenes updates on upcoming projects.

YouTube | Instagram| Facebook

@healthyinheart

Pinterest

@healthyinheart1

Join the Sabbath Table Gathering

A weekly space of peace, Scripture, reflection, shared learning, and social connection.

We gather to slow down, honor the rhythm YHVH built into creation, and get to know one another. We talk about whatever subject comes up.

Everyone is welcome — whether you're exploring Sabbath for the first time or restoring it in your home. To request an invite:

https://healthyinheart.com/contact-me-about-our-sabbath-table-gathering

The RISE™ Momentum Circle

If you desire deeper transformation, the RISE Circle offers guided group discussion rooted in whole-being wellness:

Rooted • Intentional • Strong • Energized

Together we grow in identity, emotional strength, nourishing rhythms, and whole-being wellness.

We meet on Zoom on Thursdays from 5:00 PM to 6:30 PM. To request an invite:

https://healthyinheart.com/contact-me-about-r-i-s-e

Stay Connected

Subscribe to the Healthy in Heart newsletter email list for free resources, new recipes, devotional content, early book releases, and special community invitations.

https://healthyinheart.com/subscribe

You don't have to walk toward wholeness alone.

Join us — and step into a community shaped by truth, simplicity, joy, and shalom.

Explore More

Your journey doesn't end here. If these pages have spoken to you, I'd love to walk further with you. My online store is filled with resources created to nourish your identity, strengthen your spirit, and support whole-being wellness—books that deepen your walk, journals that guide your reflection, R.I.S.E.–themed shirts and home goods that encourage you daily, and handmade items crafted with prayer and purpose.

Every product is designed to remind you of who you are and Who walks with you.
Come see what's waiting for you at **HealthyInHeart.com**

Shop Healthy in Heart Store

Each week, I release new blog articles and plant-based recipes designed to support your health, healing, identity, and whole-being wellness. From emotional and spiritual encouragement to practical nourishment for your body, these writings are meant to walk with you—one small step at a time.

You'll find teachings on R.I.S.E. principles, identity and worth, emotional healing, Hebraic roots, and simple homemade recipes that help you thrive.

Join me at HealthyInHeart.com/blog for weekly encouragement, truth, and nourishment for both body and soul. Subscribe to my newsletter by following this QR code where you can keep up-to-date on my most recent posts, new books, and monthly updates.

Sign up for the Newsletter!

The Healthy in Heart Library

The Daniel Fast 21-Day Meal Plan: Simple Plant-Based Nourishment for Mind, Body, & Spirit
Eat Well. Pray Deep. Stand Strong.

Books in the Series

Book 1- *The Eden Way*™: *Reclaiming Body, Mind, and Spirit Through the Creator's Original Design*

Book 2 -*The Eden Way*™ *Journal: 49-Days to Reset Body, Mind, and Spirit*

   (Companion to Book 1)

Books in the Series

RISE™ Wellness Journal—Rooted, Intentional, Strong, Energized: Embrace One Year of Habits, Healing, and Hope

RISE™ The Beginning of Balance—How Rooted, Intentional, Strong, and Energized Living Transforms the Whole Self: A Framework for Whole-Being Wellness

The Beginning of Balance Chronicles: The Lived Record of Learning to Inhabit RISE™

The RISE™ Circle of Wholeness Collection

   Identity & Worth Volume 1

   RISE™ Identity & Worth Living a Rooted, Intentional, Strong, and Energized Life—Volume 1

   RISE™ Identity & Worth Journal: A 12-Week Journey to a Rooted, Intentional, Strong, and Energized Life—Volume 1 (Companion to Identity & Worth, Volume 1)

Books in the Series

The Little Keepers of the Garden™: Seeds of Truth Collection

Seeds of Truth Activity Book: The Little Keepers of the Garden™ Series

Explore all titles and resources at HealthyInHeart.com

If This Journal Supported You…

If these pages helped you slow down, listen more closely, or tangibly reconnect with truth, thank you for showing up for yourself.

Many people find this journal because someone else took a moment to say, "This helped me."

If you feel comfortable, your reflection—no matter how brief—may be the encouragement someone else needs to begin their own journey.

You're welcome to share a few words wherever you usually discover books or journals, such as Amazon, Goodreads, or HealthyInHeart.com.

Your experience matters.

Your voice matters.

And your honesty may help someone else take their next step toward healing.

Thank you for choosing presence, reflection, and care.

With appreciation,

Angel Tate Keaton

www.ingramcontent.com/pod-product-compliance
Lightning Source LLC
Chambersburg PA
CBHW081658120626
46550CB00010B/2935